KIT~BAG

KIT-BAG

Don Grant

Arthur Barker Limited, London
A subsidiary of Weidenfeld (Publishers) Limited

Published in Great Britain by
Arthur Barker Ltd
91 Clapham High Street
London SW4 7T4

Copyright © 1982 by Don Grant
Introduction © Jilly Cooper

Conceived and produced by
Jay Landesman Ltd.

ISBN 0 213 16834 0

Printed in Great Britain by
Butler and Tanner Ltd.

To famous Amos

INTRODUCTION

Although there has been a plethora of funny cat books recently, none has charmed me quite so much as this one. I have admired Don Grant's work for some time; we had enormous fun working together when he illustrated my anthology, *The British In Love*, and I am delighted to have an opportunity to introduce *Kit-Bag*.

When I first met Don he was living in a large house in Putney. Being an artist, he worked at home, and his sole companion during the day, when every one else was out at school or at work, was a large black and white tom cat called Amos. I remember dropping in one morning before Christmas and finding Don solemnly drinking his way through a bottle of Dom Perignon, and Amos devouring a plate of smoked salmon. They were having, Don explained, their office party. Sadly Amos pussed away at a great age last year, but it seems fitting that *Kit-Bag* should be dedicated to such a noble and idiosyncratic beast.

I myself have always lived in cat-loving houses. When I was a child there was always a fat over-indulged tom living on filet steak and taking a swipe at the ankles of any one who passed. My husband's family once had seventeen cats, and a few years after my husband and I married, our own cat population swelled to twenty-one, making the house smell like the zoo, but at least discouraging the droppers-in.

When I started writing for *The Sunday Times* therefore relying heavily on local colour, a lot of my time was spent making atrocious cat puns. Indeed I think it was Siné who started the whole punning craze, from whom many of us caught the disease. Don Grant however not only has the advantage of drawing cats quite beautifully, but also of having a truly original mind. He has managed to avoid the pitfalls of repeating the same old jokes all over again.

Cats by their very nature suggest subtlety and wisdom. To that extent they are great deceivers for I have never found them either subtle or wise, just opportunistic, and rather thick. Perhaps the poet Tessimond was right when he wrote:

"Cats, no less liquid than their shadows,
Offer no angles to the wind.
They slip diminished, neat, through loopholes
Less than themselves . . ."

The poem ends ". . . they are seldom owned till shot and skinned," a feeling more in keeping with some of the black, or tabby humour to be found in Don's book.

My own cats will probably not forgive me for writing about their kind in this way. As they gaze balefully out of the window at the birds they are too lazy to catch or watch the goldfish aimlessly swimming to and fro in their tank, (known in our household as the cat's television) I have no idea what they are thinking. I would prefer to invent attributes and opinions to them; to watch them gliding silently about the house on unplanned errands, or sitting on the unplayed grand piano in shafts of sunlight; inscrutable furry ornaments.

In *Kit-Bag* Don manages to catch many aspects of cat character without being either too whimsical, or too savage. He too has realised that you can make them do or be anything you wish in your mind. They will only respond with a flick of the tail, a gleam in the eye, and a disdainful lick at their private parts, and you still won't be any nearer understanding them. There is probably very little to understand. Hence they are the ideal subjects for such transmogrification.

JILLY COOPER

CATCHWORDS

CATEGORY

căt′achr|ēs′ĭs (-k-), *n.* a figure by which one word is wrongly used for another. [Gr. *katachrēsis,* misuse.]

dog

CATHEDRAL

CATHOLIC

CATACLYSM

EXPLODING THE FIRST A·TOMIC BOMB

CATASTROPHIES

The cat's whiskies

Catatonic

CATKIN
(PUSSY WILLOW)

KIT·BAG

BUREAUCAT

THE SEVEN
DEADLY
SINS

GLUTTONY

SLOTH

AVARICE

LUST

ENVY

PRIDE

CATALOGUE

THE UNITED CATS OF AMERICA

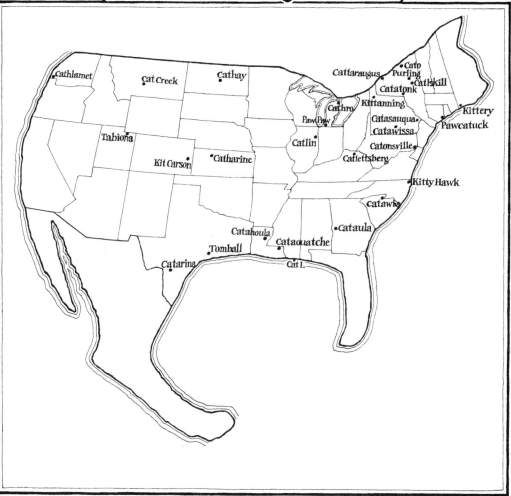

Cathlamet
Cat Creek
Cathay
Cattaraugus
Cato
Purling
Catskill
Catatonk
Cathro
Kittanning
Paw Paw
Catasauqua
Kittery
Pawcatuck
Tabiona
Catawissa
Catlin
Catonsville
Catharine
Caflettsberg
Kit Carson
Kitty Hawk
Catawba
Catahoula
Cataula
Tomball
Cataouatche
Catarina
Cat I.

MANX CAT

WOMANX CAT

There's only one thing worse than raining cats and dogs
— and that's hailing taxis.

GIANTS
OF RUSSIAN LITERATURE

PUSSKIN DOGSTOEVSKY

How to draw a capital CAT in the Roman style with the aid of geometrical instruments

As shown in the figure the body of the cat is drawn as a circle which has its major axis vertical, e_1e. To construct the tail, set off a point f midway between a and b and from f draw a line to e at the end of the major axis. Produce this this line until it intersects at g, a line drawn parallel to bc and 3 spaces below it. The curved part of the tail is tangent to eg at g, the lowest point on the curve being at a distance of 1 space from hi, while its end j is 5 spaces beyond the line cd, produced. Through the point k, 1 space above the base line, draw a line ki parallel to eg and continue it into the curve ij. The head is a circle half the diameter of the body, with its centre q ⅛ of the radius above the top of the arc described by the larger circle at r. The ears are drawn by extending the radii lm and ln until they intersect the lines pm and on at 32° from the horizontal.

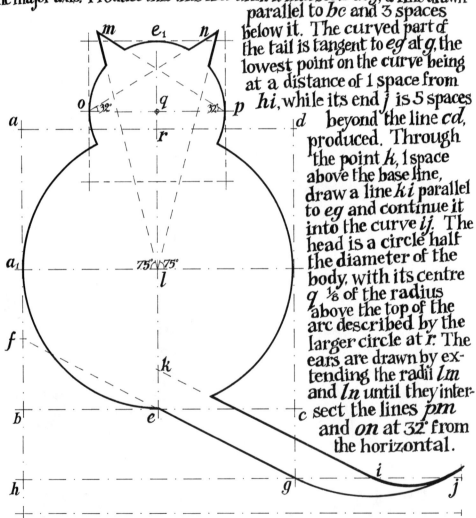

N.B. To draw a Sans Serif cat follow the instructions above exactly, but exclude the tail. cf. Manx cat.

Reprinted from 'Principia Cathematica' by Bertrand 'Jack' Russell

BEE-LINE

FELINE.

QUEEN of SPAYED

CATHODE

Paw
Catch
Claw
Scratch
Silk
Fur
Milk
Purr

IN LOVING MEMORY OF
TIDDLES
WHO WENT THROUGH THE
GREAT CAT-DOOR IN THE SKY
TO THE LAND OF MILK AND TUNNY

KITSCH

THE HARE & THE TORTOISESHELL

Popular misconceptions regarding Aesop's Fables. No.3

You can't be the cat's whiskers
if you don't let your hare down

THE STARTLING DIFFERENCE BETWEEN
A COMMA AND A CAT

A COMMA
has its pause at the
end of its clause

A CAT
has its claws at the
end of its paws

Miaow Tse-tung

AUTOMATOM

THE CAT SAT ONOMATOPOEICALLY TO MUSE

THE NINE MUSES

EUTERPE
The Muse of Music

ERATO
The Muse of Erotic Poetry

THALIA
The Muse of Comedy

MELPOMENE
The Muse of Tragedy

Tabby, or not tabby: that is the question
Whether 'tis nobler in the mind to suffer
The slings and arrows of outrageous fortunes
Or take arms against a sea of troubles
And buy a puss to end them? To die, to sleep;
No more; and by a sleep to say we end
The heart-ache and the thousand natural shocks
That flesh is heir to, 'tis a consummation
Devoutly to be wish'd. To die, to sleep,
To sleep, perchance the cream; ay there's the rub
Purr in that sleep of death what dreams may come
When we have shuffled off this mortal coil,
Must give us paws.

CLIO
The Muse of History

POLYHYMNIA
The Muse of Song

♫ O FOR THE WINGS,
FOR THE WINGS
OF A DOVE...♫

SAUTÉED GENTLY IN WHITE WINE WITH GARLIC, BASIL, MUSHROOMS AND JUNIPER BERRIES.

CALLIOPE
The Muse of Epic Poetry

HOMER
SWEET
HOMER

TERPSICHORE
The Muse of Song and Dance

URANIA
The Muse of Astronomy

METRO GOLDWYN MIAOWER

Proudly Present...

Kit Kong

Micky Meows

It is a far far better
thing that I do, than
I have ever done.

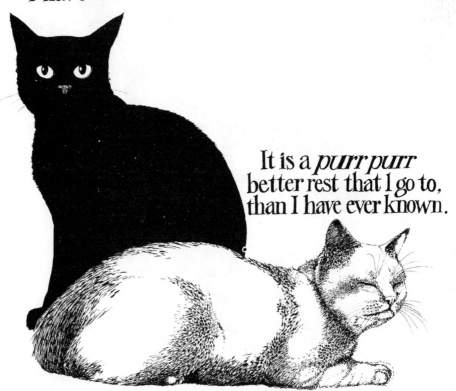

It is a *purr purr*
better rest that I go to,
than I have ever known.

A Tale of Two Kitties

Tailpiece
(or the one-eyed cat walking backwards)

Tailpiece
(or the one-eyed cat walking backwards)